Material Matters

Metals

Terry Jennings

Chrysalis Children's Books

First published in the UK in 2003 by
🌀 Chrysalis Children's Books
64 Brewery Road
London N7 9NT

© Chrysalis Books Plc 2003

Text by Terry Jennings

ISBN 1-84138-936-6

British Library Cataloguing in Publication Data
for this book is available from the British Library.

A Belitha Book

Editorial Manager: Joyce Bentley
Series Editor: Sarah Nunn
Design: Stonecastle Graphics Ltd
Picture Researcher: Paul Turner

Printed in China

10 9 8 7 6 5 4 3 2 1

Picture credits:
Alcan: pages 12, 13 (below).
Anglo American: pages 1, 8, 25 (top and below).
Caffeinebuzz: page 9 (top).
Corbis: page 14 © Christie's Images/Corbis.
Corus: page 11 (below).
Roddy Paine Photographic Studios: pages 4 (top), 5, 6 (below), 9 (below), 15, 21, 28-29.
Spectrum Colour Library: pages 4 (below), 13 (top), 19 (below).
Stonecastle Graphics: pages 22, 23 (top), 25 (centre).
Sylvia Cordaiy Photo Library: pages 10, 19 (top), 24.
Terry Jennings: pages 6 (top), 7 (top and below), 20, 23 (below).

Contents

Everyday metals

You probably touch something made of **metal** every day. It might be a knife, a door handle, a tap, a spoon, a coin, or even a bicycle or car.

Coins are made of metals such as copper and nickel.

This aircraft is being made from a lightweight metal called aluminium.

4

These saucepans are made of a special kind of steel that will not **rust**.

Most metals are strong and hard **materials**. They feel ~~cold~~ ↑ *in glossary* them. ____ sound when you hit them. Many metals are shiny when new. Metals can be made into many different shapes.

There are about 70 different kinds of metal. The metals we use most are iron, steel, aluminium and copper.

5

Where do metals come from?

Most of the metals we use come from rocks. Rocks with lots of metal in them are called **ores**.

A piece of pure gold as it was dug from the ground.

Although this looks like gold, fool's gold is really one kind of iron ore.

South Africa produces three-quarters of the world's gold.

Gold is different because it is found as the pure metal. Tiny pieces of gold are sometimes washed out of rocks into streams and rivers. Most gold, though, is found deep underground in countries such as South Africa, Australia and Russia.

This is one kind of iron ore.

A piece of aluminium ore from Canada.

Mining metals

The rocks called ores are dug up in several ways. The ores of copper, iron and aluminium are sometimes found near the surface. The ore is broken up with **drills** or **explosives**.

A huge copper **mine** in America.

Mining deep underground for gold in South Africa.

Some other metal ores are found deep underground. Long tunnels are dug down to reach them. Drills or special cutters break up the ore. The ore is brought out of the mine on small trains or on moving belts.

Copper ore

The world's deepest mine is in South Africa. It is over 3.5 kilometres deep.

Iron and steel

Iron and steel are two of the most important metals we use. Most of the iron is turned into steel. Steel is stronger than iron. It is used to make bridges, ships, cars, cranes and many other large machines and buildings.

Ironbridge was the world's first bridge made from iron. It was built in Shropshire, England in 1779.

To make iron, the iron ore has to be heated in a big oven, or **furnace**. While the iron is still runny, or **molten**, it goes into another furnace. There it is turned into steel.

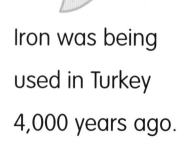

Molten steel being poured while it is still runny.

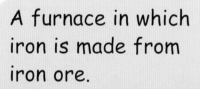

A furnace in which iron is made from iron ore.

Iron was being used in Turkey 4,000 years ago.

11

Copper and aluminium

Copper is a reddish-coloured metal. Copper pipes do not rust or **rot**, and they can be easily bent. Copper pipes are used to carry hot and cold water in buildings.

Copper was first mined and used more than 7,000 years ago.

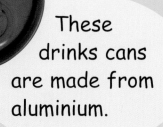

These drinks cans are made from aluminium.

Aluminium is a very lightweight, silvery-coloured metal. Some bottle tops and drinks cans are made from aluminium. Very thin sheets of aluminium are used to cover chocolate bars.

New copper pipes being stacked at the factory where they were made.

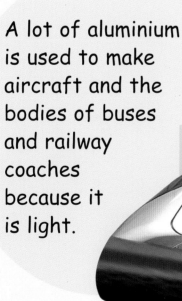

A lot of aluminium is used to make aircraft and the bodies of buses and railway coaches because it is light.

Mixing metals

Some metals have to be made stronger or harder before they can be used. This is done by adding another substance to the molten metal. A metal with another substance added to it is called an **alloy**.

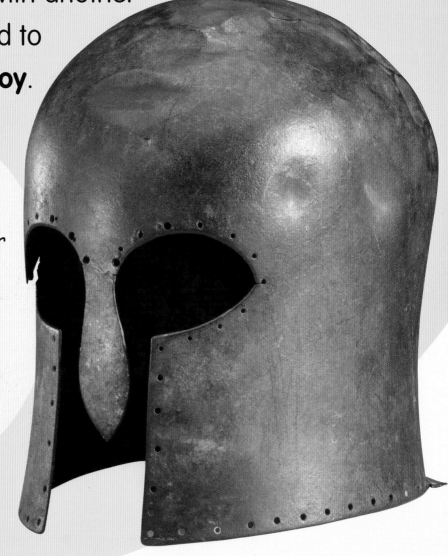

This bronze helmet was worn by a Greek soldier more than 2,000 years ago. Bronze is made by mixing together two weaker metals, copper and tin.

Brass is copper with the metal zinc added. Brass is often used for ornaments and door handles.

Stainless steel is steel with the metals chromium and nickel added. It is used for garden tools, saucepans, and knives, forks and spoons because it does not rust.

Silver and copper coins are not made of pure metals. Instead they are alloys, usually of the metals copper and nickel.

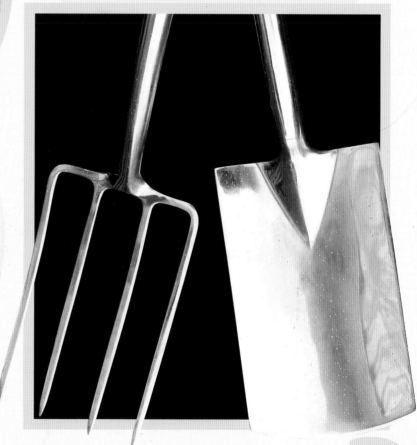

shaping metals

Pouring molten metal into a shape called a **mould**.

Although metals are hard and strong, they can be shaped. As a metal is heated, it becomes softer and can be shaped when it is red-hot by using powerful machines.

Coins, bottle tops and can lids are stamped from big sheets of metal. Some car engine parts are made by pouring molten metal into a shape called a mould. When the metal cools it sets hard in the shape of the mould.

Steel, and many other metals, can be rolled out into thin sheets when they are red-hot.

Cutting and joining metals

Some small pieces of metal can be cut with a special saw. Larger pieces of metal are cut with a narrow jet of very hot flame. The flame melts the metal and cuts it.

A welder joining two pieces of metal. The pieces have been heated and softened using a very hot flame.

It is possible to **weld** pieces of metal underwater.

The tiny metal parts of a computer or television set are joined with a soft alloy of tin.

Sometimes **bolts** or **rivets** are used to join pieces of metal together. Often the edges of the two pieces of metal are melted and then stuck together before they cool. This is called welding.

This man is using a very powerful beam of light, called a laser beam, to cut metal.

19

Metals and electricity

Metals let electricity pass through them easily. That is why the wires that carry electricity are made of metals such as copper or aluminium.

NEVER touch electric sockets, plugs or wires.

The thick wires on this electricity pylon are made of aluminium.

20

The copper wires inside an electrical plug carry electricity.

Electricity can be dangerous, so the metals carrying electricity are covered with plastic or rubber. Electricity cannot pass through plastic or rubber, so covering plugs, sockets and wires with these materials makes them safe for us to use.

Metals such as lead, zinc, nickel and cadmium are used in electrical batteries.

21

Rusting and tarnishing

Many metals change colour in moist air. Iron and steel become covered in reddish-brown rust. Copper metal turns green in moist air, while silver turns black. We say copper and silver **tarnish**.

The metal mercury is unusual because it is a metal that takes the form of a silver liquid even before it is heated.

Rust looks nasty and weakens metal objects because the metal is gradually eaten away.

To keep moist air away from iron, steel and copper, we often paint them or coat them with another substance. Tin cans are not really made of tin. They are made of thin sheets of steel with a coating of tin on the outside. The tin stops the steel from rusting.

The steel parts of this car are covered with a shiny metal called chromium. Chromium does not rust.

A copper roof goes green in moist air.

precious metals

Gold, silver and platinum are called **precious** metals because they are beautiful and rare. It is difficult and expensive to obtain them from the ground.

It is possible to beat gold into a sheet so thin that you can see through it.

This man is searching, or panning, for pieces of gold in a mountain stream.

Gold does not rust or tarnish. It is mainly used to make jewellery and ornaments.

Platinum is used in jewellery and in the exhausts of cars to help remove harmful substances. Silver is used mainly in jewellery and ornaments. Chemicals containing silver are used to make films for cameras. Both gold and silver were once used to make coins.

A gold mine in South Africa.

Recycling metals

It takes a lot of **fuel** or electricity to obtain metals. Large holes are left in the ground where the metals or their ores were dug out. These holes spoil the countryside.

If we collect old drinks cans, new objects can be made from them.

One day we will have taken all the metals out of the ground, so we must use them carefully. It is cheaper and better for our world to **recycle** metals, rather than to go on producing new ones.

Nearly half of the steel in a new car may have come from old cars that have been recycled.

Most of the metal in these old cars can be recycled.

Do it yourself

Magnets and metals

Some metals, such as iron, steel and nickel, stick to a magnet. Other metals, such as aluminium, do not.

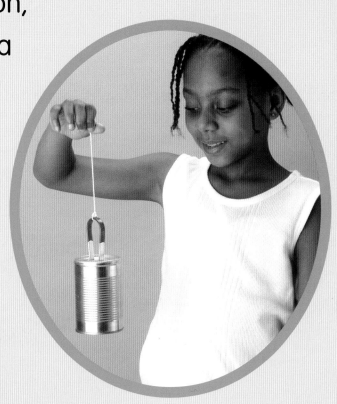

1 Collect some clean drinks cans. They are usually made of aluminium or steel.
2 See which you can pick up using a magnet.
3 The ones that stick are made of steel. The ones that do not, are made of aluminium.

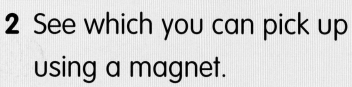

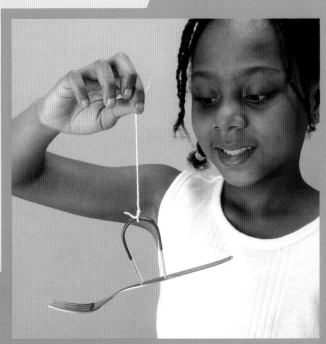

4 Now test some other metal objects to see which stick to a magnet.

Glossary

alloy A metal formed from a mixture of a metal and another substance.

bolt A thick metal pin for joining things together.

drill A tool for making holes.

explosive A substance, such as gunpowder or dynamite, that will explode.

fuel Any material, such as coal, oil or gas, that will burn and produce heat.

furnace An oven in which great heat can be produced.

materials The substances from which things are made.

metal A hard, shiny substance that melts when it is very hot.

mine A place where metals, coal and other materials are dug out of the ground.

molten Something that has turned into a liquid because it has been heated is said to be molten.

mould A container for making things set in the shape that is wanted.

ore A rock with metal in it.

precious Very valuable.

recycle To treat waste material so that it can be used again.

rivet A strong metal pin for holding pieces of metal together.

rot To go soft or bad so that the object is useless.

rust A red or brown substance that forms on iron or steel when it is in damp air.

tarnish When a metal loses its brightness.

weld To join two pieces of metal together by using heat.

Index